THE PINKO COMMIE DYKE

ALSO BY JULIE R. ENSZER

Avowed

Lilith's Demons

Sisterhood

Handmade Love

EDITED BY JULIE R. ENSZER

Fire-Rimmed Eden: Selected Poems by Lynn Lonidier

OutWrite: The Speeches that Shaped LGBTQ Literary Culture with Elena Gross

Sister Love: The Letters of Audre Lorde and Pat Parker 1974-1989

The Complete Works of Pat Parker

Milk & Honey: A Celebration of Jewish Lesbian Poetry

THE PINKO COMMIE DYKE

POEMS FROM A LEFTIST LESBIAN CABAL

JULIE R. ENSZER
ILLUSTRATIONS BY **ISABEL CLARE PAUL**

INDOLENT BOOKS

© 2024 Julie R. Enszer and Isabel Clare Paul
All Rights Reserved
book design: adam b. bohannon
Book editor: Michael Broder

www.indolentbooks.com
Indolent Books
209 Madison Street
Brooklyn, NY 11216

ISBN: 9781945023316

Special thanks to Epic Sponsor Megan Chinburg
for helping to fund the production of this book.

For Kim

Neither Commie
Nor Pinko

Always My First
My Last
My Best Dyke

CONTENTS

THE PINKO COMMIE DYKE HIJACKS 3
THE PINKO COMMIE DYKE SLEEPS 5
THE PINKO COMMIE DYKE RETURNS 6
THE PINKO COMMIE DYKE FIRES 9
THE PINKO COMMIE DYKE CARRIES 11
THE PINKO COMMIE DYKE BEATS 13
THE PINKO COMMIE DYKE EJACULATES 14
THE PINKO COMMIE DYKE PUNCHES 16
THE PINKO COMMIE DYKE INFILTRATES 18
THE PINKO COMMIE DYKE SMASHES 22
THE PINKO COMMIE DYKE HIRES 24
THE PINKO COMMIE DYKE SHOOTS 26
THE PINKO COMMIE DYKE PLOTS 29
THE PINKO COMMIE DYKE CHANTS 31
THE PINKO COMMIE DYKE REJECTS 35
THE PINKO COMMIE DYKE KILLS 37
THE PINKO COMMIE DYKE PACKS 39
THE PINKO COMMIE DYKE THOUGHT 40
THE PINKO COMMIE DYKE SHOPS 43
THE PINKO COMMIE DYKE ARMS 45
THE PINKO COMMIE DYKE VISITS 48
THE PINKO COMMIE DYKE HOT RODS 49
THE PINKO COMMIE DYKE READS 53
THE PINKO COMMIE DYKE BRUSHES 55
THE PINKO COMMIE DYKE TOURS 56
THE PINKO COMMIE DYKE LIVES 58
THE PINKO COMMIE DYKE RAGES 59

THE PINKO COMMIE DYKE COVETS   61
THE PINKO COMMIE DYKE PLANTS   63
THE PINKO COMMIE DYKE WANTS   64
THE PINKO COMMIE DYKE WONDERS   66
THE PINKO COMMIE DYKE CULTIVATES   69
THE PINKO COMMIE DYKE DESPISES   70
THE PINKO COMMIE DYKE TESTS   71
THE PINKO COMMIE DYKE PEGS   74
THE PINKO COMMIE DYKE DEMONSTRATES   77

THE PINKO COMMIE DYKE

THE PINKO COMMIE DYKE HIJACKS

the commercial airwaves
with a souped up computer
a black digital box and
a broken down microphone
that sits limp in its stand
until she places her hand
at its base and presses
her lips to its metal mesh

electrified
the whole contraption
broadcasts her words
her voice
her shows
over the air and into a
thousand tiny radios
across the region
across the nation

first she kidnaps an alt-right
talk radio station
seizing control to
broadcast lesbian folk music:
Cris and Holly and Melanie
and Bitch and Ferron
Then old recordings of Lea Delaria
and audiotaped shows

from femorist Kate Clinton
she imagines this music
these stand up routines
these objects of lesbian culture
transforming racist listeners
into peace-loving
woman-loving comrades

When she has exhausted
her lesbian supply of mp3s
and discs and tapes
she takes to the airwaves directly
the pinko commie dyke
speaks and shouts and coos
and questions and posits
then takes calls
interlocuting with people
angry about queers
and bosses and losses
of jobs and opportunity

she is startled:

they have more in common
than she ever imagined

THE PINKO COMMIE DYKE SLEEPS

next to the big fierce dog
who bit another dog
and is banned from living in Maryland
he is large
his bark is deep
his jaw strong
he sleeps next to the pinko commie dyke
his mouth at her feet
his rump near her belly
his coat warms her

in the world he is ferocious
in bed he cuddles
she dreams of waking
with his strength
of baring her teeth to enemies
of growling
of snapping
she wants to be fierce
she wants people
to cower when they see her
she wants to bite

THE PINKO COMMIE DYKE RETURNS

to the place where the idea
of being a pinko commie dyke
first entered her mind

to where *Heresies*
a feminist art journal
arrived in the mail

Who knows how
she a fifteen-year-old
in Saginaw Michigan

found *Heresies* to subscribe
(yes she supported
Geraldine Ferraro for Vice President

but in retrospect she knows
that is not what brought
Heresies into her home)

The feminists operating
Post Office Box 766
at the Canal Street Station

(many years later
she would visit that spot
her step more sprightly thinking

how those Heretics trod
the same path) mailed her
Issue 20 with a list

of epithets for
feminists on the cover
culminating with

castrating bitches
commie sluts
pinko dykes

Holding that issue
reading those words at fifteen
she knew who she wanted to be

THE PINKO COMMIE DYKE FIRES

a shot gun out behind a barn
on the farm near where her cousin lives

After all these years
of quiet east coast pacifism
liberal opposition to fire arms
she wonders could she own a shot gun?
Would she shoot to defend her family?
Could she learn to look down
the barrel to the enemy? Aim?
Inhale then exhale?
Gently squeeze the trigger?

In first practice
she hits paper
every time

After handling
an array of rifles and shot guns
she fancies a twenty gauge
not too heavy
not too light
comfortable in her hands
She can imagine owning it
buying ammo
set
load

aim
shoot

She no longer wonders:
she can take up arms
against a sea of troubles
and by defending herself
end them

THE PINKO COMMIE DYKE CARRIES

a union card opposite her driver's license
in the wallet of her imagination
Thick black leather softened from age
worn by years of use attached
to a belt loop in her Levis
with a thick silver chain
as though she is
an old school butch

The truth is she has never
punched in on a time clock
never labored on a shop floor
never sat in a line of automated machinery
repeating one small task again and again
a break every two hours for fifteen minutes
lunch for thirty in the middle of the day

Her grandmother also never carried a union card
For a few years she worked at Lufkin Rule
makers of yard sticks and rulers
on the line grandma and the other girls
cut wood for measures
stamped them with precision
manipulating heavy metal machines
with their feet
One day the woman sitting next to grandma
slipped

the machine sliced her leg at the ankle
her foot fell to the floor
grandma left that job a few weeks later
for the pickle factory
there the greatest danger
was scalding water
but it was never too hot
that the skin would not heal

The pinko commie dyke has never done work
that endangers
her fingers and toes
her hands and feet
She wonders
Is such labor required to be a commie?
Is a union card?
What if she is not in fact proletariat?
What if she is bourgeoisie?

THE PINKO COMMIE DYKE BEATS

back all manner of supremacy:
aggressions—micro and macro—that assert
straight white male superiority
the primacy of markets
identities derived from annual incomes and bank balances.
Every day she delivers
multiple critiques of accepted knowledge
feminist evaluation
provocative new frameworks
queer rejoinders
She demands a reconsideration
of family relationships
of how we organize our daily lives
This work is the labor of a lifetime
Every day her mind engages
her tongue is sharp
alternating between bitter and caustic
but in the mornings
before the barrage of battle
she eats blueberries
for breakfast with fresh whipped cream
Before the day beats her down
she fills her mouth with sweetness

THE PINKO COMMIE DYKE EJACULATES

clear liquid as she comes
standing on her knees
her clitoris swollen
her nipples erect
that guttural *yes*
emerges multiply
from the back of her throat
as come streams from her pussy
down her legs
onto dry clean sheets
warm liquid from all the pleasures of sex
drenches her body her bed
then cools as she collapses
into the warm wet spot
that soon becomes cold
prompting her to roll away
wait for the sheets to dry
leaving only a faint musky odor
from deep inside: pleasure desire sex.
The pinko commie dyke muses
this may be the scent of revolution:
the smell of dried spunk on cotton sheets
Revolutionary or not
that odor drives her to stand on her knees
engorged again
begging for pleasure
for stimulation for pressure for play

pledging allegiance
to the hand mouth latex cock
of the woman coaxing
clear ejaculate to stream again

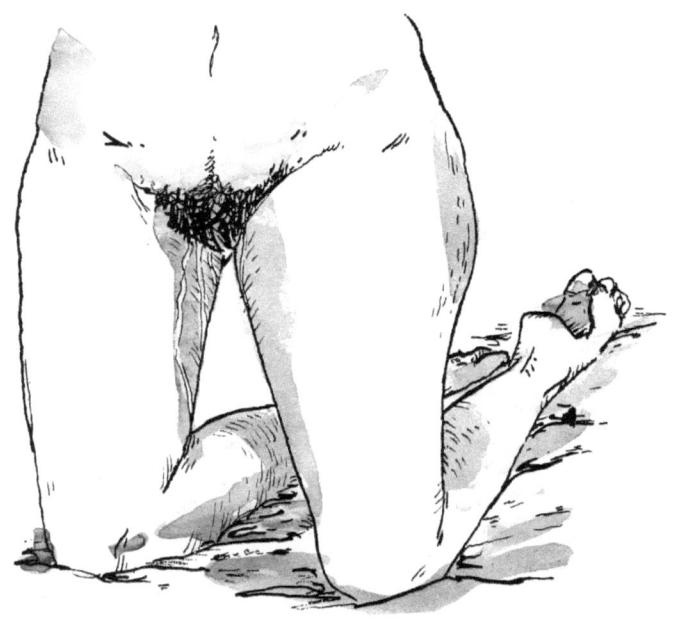

THE PINKO COMMIE DYKE PUNCHES

a Bernie Bro
all her anger distilled
into the silver rings
across three fingers
all her rage summoned
from her core to
her shoulder
her arm
her fist

She does not anticipate
the crack of her knuckles
against mandible and maxilla
the way blood and tissue
catch in silver crevices
of the rings as she swings

She denies the peace symbol
tattooed on the base of her spine
channels Valerie Solanas
imagines her hand
on a cool revolver
Warhol in the sight lines

She expects the smug smirk
atop his hipster beard
to endure after she clocks him

it does
she hates it

For a minute she knows:
Valerie's anger
Valerie's relief
Valerie's satisfaction
with her power
finally able to act on her rage
patriarchy inflicts violence
it deserves violence in turn

She does not know:
the headache from the rage
the jaw pain from the clench
the soreness in her elbow
the post-punch ache in her shoulder
the smell of blood on her fingers
the swelling of her hands
the fear from her loss of self-control

THE PINKO COMMIE DYKE INFILTRATES

the local hog club
down here at the end
of Davidson Road

Nothing more than a shack
a single electrical outlet
powers the fridge

always stocked with beer
occasionally some whisky
more often moonshine

A barn once storing seed
and equipment tucked in a corner
of Buddy's old farm

Buddy's family bought out
in the '70s when his kids
all left for the city

except Vern who stayed
living in the big house
by himself all these years

Always friendly with his cousin
Virgil who started the club
with Vern's blessing

even though Virg and his kin
were often on the wrong
side of the law

One day the sheriff
came out to warn Vern
about the potential liabilities

of letting riders gather
there on the edge
of his property

There's gonna be trouble
out there someday
the sheriff told Vern

Vern looked at the sheriff
long and hard and said
I hear ya sheriff but

no man can let another
tell him what he can and cannot
do with his property

You know that sheriff
and he did so the two sat
on the porch thirty minutes

longer as the sun sank
and the Harleys drove away
Then the sheriff got into his

squad car flipped the siren
once and went on his way
That was ten years before

the pinko commie dyke
moved into town with her
new Harley all shiny

and loud a big thrum
between her legs
At first everyone in town

thought she was a man
the Harley
the black leather jacket

crisp new Levis
One day at the club
after a long ride

quiet scrutiny revealed
her womanly breasts
No bother

They still call her buddy
at the hog club when
they gather on weekends

During the summer
they drink late into the night
until darkness overtakes

the single spot light
plugged into the other socket
near the refrigerator

In winter riders depart early
against evening chills and darkness
The pinko commie dyke knows

camaradie among hog riders
is the same whether
riding for visibility

in the streets of New York City
or riding for pleasure
along a southern holler

THE PINKO COMMIE DYKE SMASHES

goblets glasses and serving bowls
ornaments tea cups and champagne flutes
coffee mugs plates and glass chargers
green water glasses from Mexico with blue cobalt rims
and decorative blown glass *objets de art*
she smashes them all
a veritable *kristalnacht* upending power
at the local shopping mall

She knows all the fags working retail:
they leave a door unlocked
an alarm unarmed
She slips in to sack the stores
an irreverent statement
against commercialism
against the desire to own
when so many have nothing
against the impulse to entertain
while there are homeless people
to feast while some starve
to create beauty while abject poverty persists

The meanings of the pinko commie dyke's actions
are lost in news reports
anchors describe midnight vandalism
police officers finger local punks
but the pinko commie dyke knows

she waits to find others
who hear her cries of defiance
who revel in breaking glass
lashing out against capitalist heteropatriarchy
smashing capitalist covenants

THE PINKO COMMIE DYKE HIRES

a repair man from a company she found online
He is white nearly sixty and from Alabama
but living in Florida since '08
because this is where the jobs are

He has a bad knee
It buckles as he walks
down the stairs
he catches himself with the rail

When he delivers the news
the washer cannot be fixed
*too old—they don't manufacture
the parts any more—a shame*

the pinko commie dyke asks
what machine do you recommend
he looks her up and down and says
don't buy from the Koreans

*you think with an American name
they are American-made
but they are Korean—Sanyo LG
the machines look good but*

the Koreans don't make anything that lasts
he pauses and looks at her again

maybe buy a Whirlpool
The pinko commie dyke stares at the repair man

From Michigan she knows laid off
Whirlpool workers but now she realizes
she doesn't know where any appliances
are made

She imagines where ever people make appliances
the work breaks their bodies
as it broke bodies in Michigan
as work has broken the appliance repair man's body

she would like to make a connection
between those workers and the repair man
show a web of globalization
connecting—constraining—them all

but words fail her
whelp, he says, *you'll figure it out*
nothing is really good anymore
nothing is like it used to be

THE PINKO COMMIE DYKE SHOOTS

a handgun
then thinks
she can never own one
never hold it nonchalantly
in her hands as her own
never store it in a coat pocket
a purse
a holster
never stash it in her waist band
conceal it near her ankle

It is too easy
too easy to take aim
to fire
too easy
to take down a person
to injure
to claim a life

She wants to defend her home
her family

She would kill if necessary
but first she wants to intimidate
she wants to bully
she wants to threaten

she wants to prompt an aggressor to reconsider
she wants to protect

a handgun is not a weapon for conversation
so easy to squeeze the trigger
how quickly the bullet slips from the shaft
the handgun carries only one intention

the pinko commie dyke thinks
she could never own one

then she wonders
but what if I did?

THE PINKO COMMIE DYKE PLOTS

to build the proper tool
to smash patriarchy
she imagines a design
creates a schematic
builds a model to test
the first works too narrowly
dissembles only a few aspects of patrimony—
eliminates the patronym
weakens the father in traditional family structures—
but it does nothing to challenge
let alone eradicate white supremacy
and its effects on heterosexuality
are minimal
She returns to the drawing board
New plans samples prototypes
She imagines the perfect tool
mass produced in a classic union
manufacturing shop
She envisions distributing it
to young women to smash the patriarchy
to queers to wield against the heteropatriarchy
to people of color to smash white supremacy
She imagines it might even have applications to
dismantle nationalism
She wants to arm all the rabble

with a tool
to end capitalism
Muttering in front of her computer
she says
Yes Yes let's build this

THE PINKO COMMIE DYKE CHANTS

Better Blatant than Latent
the popular gay rights chant
celebrating blatant homos

as they parade down streets
wearing pride tees
sporting styled packages

and product-applied hair
while deriding latent homos
sitting on couches at home

next to their wives
The commie pinko dyke
has always been blatant—

whether by birth or by choice—
and she holds the requisite derision
for the latent

who deny hide obscure
all that is queer
embrace privilege for their own benefit

lest this conversation be intellectual
consider the commie pinko dyke's
father who came out after her mother died

When mother was alive
deriding all the queers
with a blatancy befitting

her commie pinko daughter
her father could not even conjure snide
the latent bastion of dissent

Now mother's vitriol buried
and father with a live-in lover
all is supposedly forgiven

She assumes the pose
of obedient lesbian daughter
He is just another gay daddy

but she knows his secrets:
years of silence
while other spoke

years of closeted sex
when others fucked and died
when blatant

took to the streets
appealed for basic
rights and recognition

only to be met with ridicule
mockery and violence
latent looked on

with fear and pity
Now her father basks in rights
secured by labors of others

The pinko commie dyke knows
even in family there is
no justice no peace

THE PINKO COMMIE DYKE REJECTS

beauty as a construct of patriarchy
Written on women's bodies
through constraint and enforced modification
beauty thwarts healthy sexualities and erotic desires

The pinko commie dyke hates beauty
the pain it creates for women
the need to primp and cover
to blot and pluck to suck and shape

Beauty compares Finds women wanting
She cultivates ugliness
space outside the male gaze
space where bodies can be free

Except when she reads that line by Millay
Still will I harvest beauty where it grows:
Then she believes in beauty
She wants to join Millay in a bucolic field

of flowers and fresh scents with pollinating bees
making wild honey And it is not just Millay
who fosters beauty-lust: the other day a poem
came across her desk So spare immediate

perfect and she thought *so beautiful*
The startling revelation left her breathless
gasping for air brought clarity: the pinko
commie dyke rejects beauty and she yearns for it

THE PINKO COMMIE DYKE KILLS

babies on street corners
with the steel speculum
she has been carrying
since she was nineteen
and gazing at her cervix
with a group of women

Now the Kumbaya of
body exploration has passed
and abortion docs are in demand
commanding high fees
for a simple D & C
The pinko commie dyke
helps women dilate and
evacuate their own uteri
as women have for ages
with herbs or pebbles or poultices

A thin metal line
pierces the endometrium
like rupturing the yolk
of an egg menses slither
through the cervix
down the uterine wall
sloughing that baby
into the toilet
creating a vast empty space

in the womb where
the woman now child-free
can move in
kick back
have a cocktail
and enjoy herself

The pinko commie dyke takes one life
and gives another in return

THE PINKO COMMIE DYKE PACKS

her Levis before she goes out
Not a realistic cock and balls
but a set of thick white socks
rolled and folded and stuffed
in men's underwear
She packs not to perform masculinity
but for women to see her
endowed with strength and authority
She packs not to promise penetration
though she will peg
if that is what women want
with her lavender dildo
strapped in a black leather harness
Both bodily appendages are for pleasure
for women to desire her
as she desires them
The pinko commie dyke packs
power in her pants
not for patriarchy
but for women's liberation

THE PINKO COMMIE DYKE THOUGHT

words could save us

women
queers
people of color
children

the world

Now she thinks,
Isn't that precious?

She was once young
idealistic
believed in the power of ideas
the goodness of humanity
the possibility of language to transform

those days have passed

Now she is barricading the house
gathering provisions for survival
preparing her body for battle

the opposition uses language
to bully

belittle
badger
belie
besmirch
bedevil
bolster
their case

they do not view language
as a source of transformation
as a way to remold our thinking

the enemy does not want to listen
engage in thoughtful debate
learn
change
grow
love

for the enemy
language is a weapon

to load
spray
insult
incent
provoke
prevent

dissent
enrage

language is a battle

they only will know
they have met their match
when they are staring down
a double barrel

language will never win

the pinko commie dyke knows
words cannot save us

THE PINKO COMMIE DYKE SHOPS

at a grocery store
with no organic section
no big placards that say local—
where else would food come from?—
no "farm to table" signs
nothing pesticide-free
nothing GMO-free
no raw nuts
no fermented kombucha
no unpasteurized milk
While picking up eggs and butter
the pinko commie dyke looks around
and knows all the kids—
running and jumping and crying
and wiping their hands and spit and snot
on their mothers' shirts and pants—
have been vaccinated to strengthen
the pack and survived and on occasion
each one of them have been swatted
on their bottoms for bad behavior
Here all the fruit and vegetables are fresh
Here all the choices are constrained
but not complicated by imagined
world-changing consequences
The pinko commie dyke picks up
romaine lettuce and hummus

black olives and diet Coke
She dines as she shops
with people without pretension

THE PINKO COMMIE DYKE ARMS

prostitutes and hookers and ladies of the night
with stolen handguns and a small reprinted
pamphlet about Joann Little the woman
who killed the prison guard who raped her

the pinko commie dyke feels sure the pamphlet
is quickly discarded but that powerful untraceable weapon
its serial number ground down
with a full clip of ammunition

women hold on to it
use it when necessary
the pinko commie dyke later hears of her work
in newspaper clippings and televised reports

men's dead bodies found in the seediest
parts of town
after she has visited
after she has sat with ladies

a single bullet wound to the head
eight shots to the torso—
overkill so that the heart explodes—
more than one woman killed a john by blowing

off his balls but one spunky gal
added her own flourish—

cut off his cock
and put it in his own mouth—

the commie pinko dyke recoils from knives
they can turn too easily on the women she wants to aid
still she delights in artful adaptations
women bring to this subversive revolution

arming women to pick off men one by one
is not a broad strategy for change
but oh how satisfying
for the woman who pulls the trigger

THE PINKO COMMIE DYKE VISITS

welding shops near her home
where they fix car frames
fabricate industrial machines
and repair household items
She investigates mold making
for her smashing tool
An early model was too heavy
for young women to wield with ease
She worried they might
hurt themselves or others
The one made from cheap
aluminum was too light
It might tamp down sexism
but could never smash anything
let alone the all powerful patriarchy
She tries to explain all of this
to the men in the shop
The owner says
We can make whatever you want ma'am
Anything is possible just bring us a model
The commie pinko dyke nods
Yes Yes of course
They do not understand:
many have tried but none
have fashioned the weapon
to deliver a final fatal blow
ending patriarchy
freeing women to rise

THE PINKO COMMIE DYKE HOT RODS

in an old Mustang convertible
red with a tan leather interior
the hood, covering all those horses
that power her down the street
gleams in the sunlight
She keeps it clean so when
she drives fast no stray papers—
napkins fast food receipts—
fly up from the wheel wells
like white flags signaling surrender
The pinko commie dyke
never surrenders
On sunny afternoons
she cranks up the radio
plays songs from the 1980s
as if they were popular still
She releases her long hair
from its usual bun
She sings aloud to her jams
and for a minute just
a minute her hair blowing
in the wind lip syncing
don't you forget about me
she feels care free
She thinks nothing
in the world matters
And for her nothing does:

no police officers follow
her on freeways or
in private developments
She speeds around town
unfettered by cops
She will not be pulled from
her car and bludgeoned to death
She will not be shot
pulling out her license
She could drive blissfully into eternity
never attracting attention
from the fuzz but she won't
She stops
She turns down the radio
Pins back her hair
She has arrived at her meeting
to plan a protest
She silences the fillies of her engine
Much more matters than
her jam this hot rod
the sweet fast Mustang beneath her legs

THE PINKO COMMIE DYKE READS

to children at the library
they love her purple hair
her long flowy dresses
the stories she weaves
from blank pages in a book

She holds up Caldecott
award-winners when parents
and librarians walk by
but their attention to three-
and four-year-olds is fleeting

most afternoons she reads
alone with the little ones
teaching them to laugh and cry
to shudder with fear
then hug themselves in consolation

she tells them about fairies
and trolls and the myriad
ways humans make lives
she reads them a future
of tolerance and love

of defiance and insistence
she attends to these little people

breeding love for commie pinko dykes
for a world that embraces
single old angry harridans

THE PINKO COMMIE DYKE BRUSHES

her teeth twice a day
with an $80 electric tooth brush
On the east coast everyone

has pearly whites
They brush and floss
fix and repair

Everyone has a mouthful
as though affluence repels
coffee and cigarette stains

lost teeth and dentures
In the post-industrial Midwest
plagued by job losses

a failed manufacturing economy
metropolitan deconcentration
plaque and decay settle

in people's mouths like rust
or gray grit and dust
No one here keeps

all the teeth in their head
There is no way to floss over it
Nothing can brush it away

THE PINKO COMMIE DYKE TOURS

downtown Detroit
city of her young adulthood
where she dreamed a future

She marvels at refurbished buildings
trendy restaurants
white people walking Woodward on a Friday night

Then at the corner of John R
she sees the "loft" where her friend lived
as an urban pioneer
They would take the old elevator
up four floors to an open space
exposed beams
an industrial wood floor
drafty floor to ceiling windows
covered inside and out with city grime
More post-industrial apocalypse
with festering health and safety issues
than aspirational Brooklyn bohemian

Oh and the rats
They were menacing
and bitter about human entry into their territory
They scattered whenever
the lights went on but not quickly

and often they looked
over their shoulders with defiance

Her friend wanted to get a gun to shoot them
but worried the whole building
would crumble from the vibrations of each blast
She lives in Los Angeles now
The pinko commie dyke lives down south

That old building has Lululemon at street level
WeWork colonizes five floors above

Marvel at urban renewal
new life for the Motor City
but poverty and racism persist
The pinko commie dyke knows:
nothing is transformed

THE PINKO COMMIE DYKE LIVES

in a house that cost three times
the price of an average American home

it marks her privileged
home ownership precludes her

being a commie pinko any longer
she is a member of the petty bourgeoisie

though she pretends she is not
she imagines she is infiltrating wealth

studying it
preparing for the next revolution

perhaps she is
but every night

her stomach is full
every night she sleeps without fear

THE PINKO COMMIE DYKE RAGES

about white spandex
which becomes transparent when wet
as it gets from sweat in yoga classes
This morning during the 60-minute hot yoga
she looked at a young skinny white woman's
anus for the whole standing series
She could see the black hairs ringing her asshole

She would rage about women buying white spandex
but the commie pinko dyke is a radical feminist
and tired of the way everyone blames individual women
for what they wear or do not wear
how and when they complain and when and why they do not
this week in particular
has been a litany of critiques of women

the commie pinko dyke
does not want to repeat that paradigm
she knows an institutional solution is necessary:
the manufacture and distribution of white spandex
must be banned
it is a campaign she can organize
she knows other women will support it
organize and educate
yes, that is what is needed

the commie pinko dyke will turn to this project
just as soon as the Supreme Court justice nominee
is defeated
just as soon as sexual harassment is eliminated
just as soon as sexual assault is eradicated
just as soon as domestic violence is completely thwarted
just as soon as women are safe and free from violence

soon and very soon
we will have no more white spandex
in work out clothes

the pinko commie dyke knows it
soon and very soon
we are going to change the world

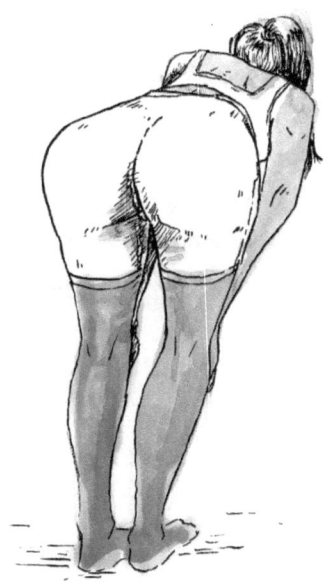

THE PINKO COMMIE DYKE COVETS

expertise
she wants to find it everywhere

She wants knowledge
complex answers
carefully crafted results from years of study and practice

She wants to surround herself with experts
a person who knows exactly how to care
for the St Augustine grass in her yard
how to encourage that grass to grow
the weeds to whither and die
how to cultivate a yard where the snakes
and possums and damselflies feast

She wants a craftsperson
to restore the arts and crafts office chair
with a broken spring and caster wheel
with black paint covering ancient oak
she wants to reclaim that chair
for daily use
to sit and twirl and recline

She wants a writing companion
who reads more than she
a mechanic who restores old cars
and is a computer whiz

a cobbler who loves shoes
and always says *I can fix this*
She wants people who immerse themselves
in the work before them
who develop specialized knowledge
people who delve deeply
know vast quantities of information
work with ideas and concepts
work with their hands and tools
know what they do not know
and know what they do know better than anyone else

The pinko commie dyke wants expertise all around her
she wants to recognize brilliance
cultivated with patience
persistence
hours of study and practice
she wants this expertise in others
with the hope that they
will recognize it in her

THE PINKO COMMIE DYKE PLANTS

lavender seeds by the dozen
They are hard to sprout
the seedlings fragile
seven fledgling filaments
transplanted into individual pots die
small brown withered strings
sit in pots of dirt on the window
Too much water?
Not enough sunlight?
Too much direct sun?
The pink commie dyke reseeds
waters
and waits
She imagines window sills
covered with pots
of blooming lavender
the house smelling like a French field
What won't she do for a purple bloom?
What won't she do for beauty?

THE PINKO COMMIE DYKE WANTS

all women to have orgasms
regularly
pleasurably
This desire is why so many lesbians
lead sexuality education classes:
they too want all women
to have great orgasms
This reality lends credence
to men's worries about lesbians
and straight women—their wives
and daughters and mothers and lovers—
lesbians want them to come
The pinko commie dyke wants
women—all women—to come
though she focuses on
one woman at a time
the one lying naked before her
on her back
legs spread
she wants her to come
when her lips
are on her labia
when her mouth
moves with her hips
when her tongue
is on her clit

this

this

this

is what the pinko commie dyke wants

THE PINKO COMMIE DYKE WONDERS

how can she love the inspector
sent by the county to check
the installation of the new propane tank?

The inspector says
I've been doing county inspections for seventeen years
was a general contractor for fifteen years before that

I know what is going on in the industry
So the fellow remodeling the bathroom
and the pinko commie lean in

They had just been discussing the national economy
They asks the inspector
Where do you see things going in the next year?

Well, he says, *it is busy right now*
but it will slow down in six to nine months
People will sit back for the elections

And of them Democrats win
I tell you
He draws closer to the two

If them Democrats win
there will be another Civil War
They look on wide-eyed

as he prattles on about the dangers
of Democrats
of the importance of the second amendment

and protecting it
the shooting range on his property
semiautomatic weapons

and how the county sheriff comes out
to shoot with him and his buddies
at the range at his house

This only the beginning
of his conversation
with the commie pinko dyke

who he clearly does not recognize as commie
or pinko
or dyke

and she wonders
How can I love this man?
It is the work of poets to love the world

the work of pinko commie dykes to love the people
especially working people
the working class

She wonders

How can I love the world if I do not love him?

then, What fails us first: people or ideology?

The propane-fired water heater works

It passes inspection

It is only a few days before she can shower with hot water

THE PINKO COMMIE DYKE CULTIVATES

large green plants
Schefflera
sweet viburnum
philodendrons
and ferns
They grow like weeds
in this hot humid climate
waxy green leaves
reaching upward to the sun
stems filling pots
new growth poking up
through sandy dirt
She likes their lushness
the languid suggestion
growth is relentless
life inevitable

THE PINKO COMMIE DYKE DESPISES

homophobia in all its manifestations
but if pressed to choose she will take
the homophobia of rural Republican
neighbors who live next to her in Florida
over the homophobia of liberal north
easterners any day because when you confront
north eastern liberals about their homophobia
they deny distract and tell you all
about their gay friend in the seventies and
how they used to all party together at the disco
and *wow weren't those great times*
or they tell you about the AIDS charity
they support early in the eighties when
no one else really cared or they natter on about
the best friend of their kid (who is not
that way though it would be fine
if they were but they are not
just as a point of fact) then they say
you are too sensitive or angry
or unreasonable or not a good role model
or just plain wrong because they are NOT
homophobic you are clearly the one with the problem
whereas the neighbors in Florida
they just don't like you and all that gay stuff
but you keep the lawn mowed and a loaded gun
so they respect you from a distance
this respect the pinko commie dyke thinks
this respect may just be the very best we can get

THE PINKO COMMIE DYKE TESTS

a labrys as a model tool
to smash patriarchy
a sentimental favorite
since lesbians co-opted
the Minoan tool
as a taliswoman
worn on a long leather cord
swaying between breasts
or strung with beads
hanging from hoop earrings

Sadly the labrys is a non-starter
the heavy double-headed axe
is dangerous when untrained
hands wield it

one woman gashed her shoulder
another gouged her knee
in an experimental environment

Next she tries a sword
It slices and splits
with strength and surety
It stops, it kills, but
it does not definitively
eliminate patriarchy

She tries a mace
which stuns and injures
but does not stop
let alone shatter
or obliterate
The battering ram
holds promise
requiring collective
action
drawing on cooperation
and communal engagement
It is effective at
knocking down barriers
opening doors
though literally only
not figuratively

Ultimately none of these objects
from the ancient tool chest
will smash the system
Maybe that is why it endures

The pinko commie dyke decides
patriarchy must not be smashed open
but cracked
like a walnut
the meat removed carefully
with a precise pick
then the shell pieced back together
not glued

but remade with molten steel
heated then poured into molds
cooled slowly to temper
the metal and fix the shell
together new and strong

The challenge is not smashing
not splitting open as Rukeyser theorized
a split does not eliminate patriarchy
and end all oppression
the challenge is constructing something new
taking that which was smashed or split
and crafting it into something useable
remaking it into something beautiful
The pinko commie dyke realizes
no single tool will do

THE PINKO COMMIE DYKE PEGS

when her lover wants
to feel the purple latex dildo
deep inside her
but she prefers it
when her lover straps it on
with the black leather harness
and puts her on her knees
to fuck her doggie style
The pinko commie dyke's pussy
sucks up that dildo
as her lover reaches around
to rub her clit
her nipples graze the cotton sheets
and she holds that loveliness
inside as her lover pumps and grinds
their thighs slap slap slap
against each other
work and play
pleasure and gender
meld into one another
slap slap moan
until finally the pinko commie dyke
comes and falls on to the bed
exhausted and happy and sated
then sometimes her lover
takes that purple cock and slides
it up inside her again

their two bodies side by side
the lover works the tool
into her warm wet space
and the pink commie dyke thinks
Oh no I cannot again
but there that stroke
against her butt
the lover's tongue upon her breast
finger on her engorged clit
they are off
working for revolution again

THE PINKO COMMIE DYKE DEMONSTRATES

for peace on Monday
welfare rights on Tuesday
economic justice on Wednesday
reproductive rights on Friday

on Thursday she volunteers at the soup kitchen
and Saturday mornings she is out at the abortion clinic
helping women safely enter

she shows up at every rally every demo
when people need a body out on the streets
for rights or to redress
wrongs
organizers just think of her
and she shows up
with her old placard.

She stores two in the garage
one says

ANOTHER
PINKO COMMIE DYKE
FOR
with a 8 ½ x 11 inch space
for a sheet of paper
sometimes white
sometimes neon pink

which she tapes on
with handwritten words

EQUALITY
JUSTICE
PEACE
MEDICARE FOR ALL
ABORTION RIGHTS
ECONOMIC EQUALITY

She writes the slogan
needed for the specific rally

The other placard is nearly the same

ANOTHER
PINKO COMMIE DYKE
AGAINST
and space for the sheet of paper

WAR
NUKES
WELFARE CUTS
PRICKS

(though she uses that one rarely)

When she lived in San Francisco
she was truly another

but in

Iowa City

Kalamazoo

Bar Harbor

Cleveland

Lexington

Denton

Tuscaloosa

Augusta

or any of the thousands of towns
across America

she is often *a* pinko commie dyke
or *the* pinko commie dyke

which is fine

Wherever she is
whatever the cause
the pinko commie dyke
is there
standing with indignation
standing with righteousness
standing with her sign
standing
she knows another era is rising

ACKNOWLEDGEMENTS

The author gratefully acknowledges these publications where poems first appeared, often in a slightly different form.

"The Pinko Commie Dyke Hires" in *Jewish Current*.
"The Pinko Commie Dyke Hot Rods" in *Gargoyle*.
"The Pinko Commie Dyke Kills" in *Impossible Archetypes*.
"The Commie Pinko Dyke Returns" in *The Quarry* at Split This Rock.

Gratitude to comrades Gerald Maa and Michael Walsh, writing buddies, constant friends. Appreciation to Jen Benka and her book *Pinko* which planted a seed for this series of poems. Always affection for the four-legged party members: Vita, Samantha, Sadie, and Alice (and the beloved ghost of Tiberius).

ABOUT THE AUTHOR

JULIE R. ENSZER, PHD, is the author of five poetry collections and editor of *OutWrite: The Speeches that Shaped LGBTQ Literary Culture, Fire-Rimmed Eden: Selected Poems by Lynn Lonidier, The Complete Works of Pat Parker,* and *Sister Love: The Letters of Audre Lorde and Pat Parker 1974-1989.* Enszer edits and publishes *Sinister Wisdom,* a multicultural lesbian literary and art journal. More at www.JulieREnszer.com.

ABOUT THE ILLUSTRATOR

ISABEL CLARE PAUL is a freelance illustrator. She was born and raised in Michigan and has a BFA Degree in Illustration from the College for Creative Studies. More at www.IsabelCPaul.com.

ABOUT INDOLENT BOOKS

Founded in 2015 as a home for poets over 50 without a first book, Indolent Books today publishes innovative, provocative, and risky books by a diverse and inclusive range of writers across genres.

www.ingramcontent.com/pod-product-compliance
Lightning Source LLC
Chambersburg PA
CBHW060537080526
44586CB00012B/771